Mar

P9-DGV-646

Kansas City, MO Public Library
00001856655198

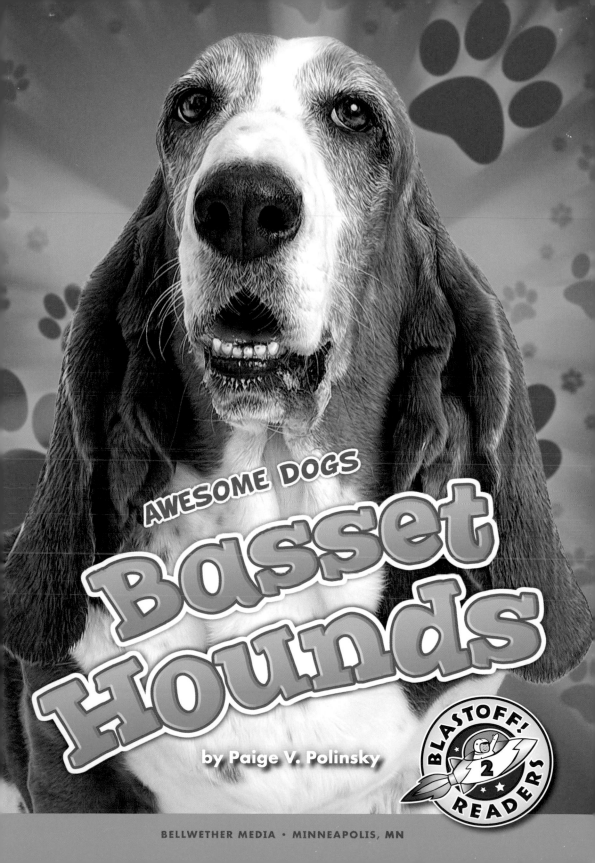

AWESOME DOGS

Basset Hounds

by Paige V. Polinsky

BLASTOFF! READERS
2

BELLWETHER MEDIA · MINNEAPOLIS, MN

Note to Librarians, Teachers, and Parents:

Blastoff! Readers are carefully developed by literacy experts and combine standards-based content with developmentally appropriate text.

Level 1 provides the most support through repetition of high-frequency words, light text, predictable sentence patterns, and strong visual support.

Level 2 offers early readers a bit more challenge through varied simple sentences, increased text load, and less repetition of high-frequency words.

Level 3 advances early-fluent readers toward fluency through increased text and concept load, less reliance on visuals, longer sentences, and more literary language.

Level 4 builds reading stamina by providing more text per page, increased use of punctuation, greater variation in sentence patterns, and increasingly challenging vocabulary.

Level 5 encourages children to move from "learning to read" to "reading to learn" by providing even more text, varied writing styles, and less familiar topics.

Whichever book is right for your reader, Blastoff! Readers are the perfect books to build confidence and encourage a love of reading that will last a lifetime!

This edition first published in 2018 by Bellwether Media, Inc.

No part of this publication may be reproduced in whole or in part without written permission of the publisher. For information regarding permission, write to Bellwether Media, Inc., Attention: Permissions Department, 5357 Penn Avenue South, Minneapolis, MN 55419.

Library of Congress Cataloging-in-Publication Data

Names: Polinsky, Paige V., author.
Title: Basset Hounds / by Paige V. Polinsky.
Description: Minneapolis, MN : Bellwether Media, Inc., 2018. | Series:
   Blastoff! Readers. Awesome Dogs | Audience: Age 5-8. | Audience: K to
   Grade 3. | Includes bibliographical references and index.
Identifiers: LCCN 2017028766 | ISBN 9781626177383 (hardcover : alk. paper) |
   ISBN 9781681034539 (ebook)
Subjects: LCSH: Basset hound–Juvenile literature.
Classification: LCC SF429.B2 P65 2018 | DDC 636.753/6–dc23
LC record available at https://lccn.loc.gov/2017028766

Text copyright © 2018 by Bellwether Media, Inc. BLASTOFF! READERS and associated logos are trademarks and/or registered trademarks of Bellwether Media, Inc. SCHOLASTIC, CHILDREN'S PRESS, and associated logos are trademarks and/or registered trademarks of Scholastic Inc., 557 Broadway, New York, NY 10012.

Editor: Betsy Rathburn   Designer: Lois Stanfield

Printed in the United States of America, North Mankato, MN.

Table of Contents

Basset hounds are calm dogs with long ears. They are great at following **scents**!

4

These friendly dogs are often called bassets.

Bassets are **stocky** dogs.
They have short legs and
long backs.

Basset Hound Profile

loose
skin

long
ears

short legs

Life Span: 10 to 12 years

Trainability:

| 1 | 2 | 3 | 4 | 5 | 6 |

Hardest to train   Easiest to train

Some can weigh up to 65 pounds
(29 kilograms)!

Basset **coats** are short and **glossy**. They can be **bi-color** or **tri-color**.

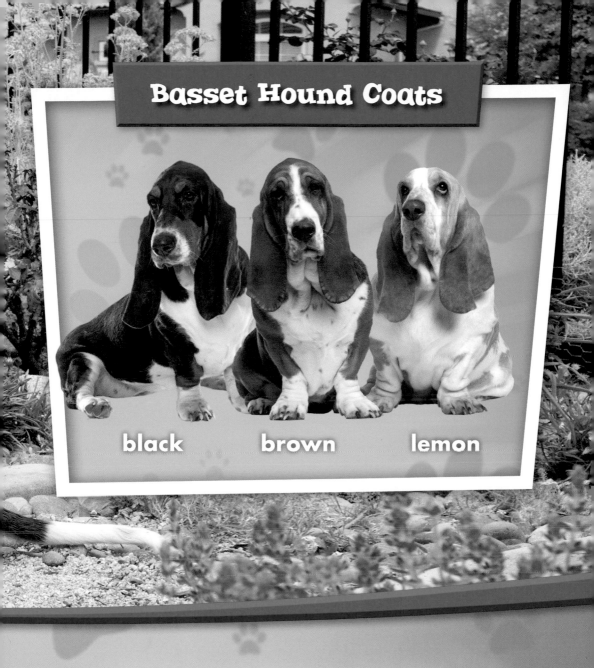

Basset Hound Coats

black   brown   lemon

Common colors are black, brown, and **lemon**. Most coats have white markings.

Bassets have loose skin. **Droopy** eyes make this **breed** look sad.

The dogs also have huge paws and long tails that point to the sky.

Bassets first came from France. They were used as hunting dogs for hundreds of years.

France

N
W E
S

These hounds got their name from the French word *bas*, or "low."

Bassets were **bred** to have long ears. These swept scents up from the ground.

The dogs' strong noses found rabbits easily. Their slow speed helped hunters follow them on foot.

Bassets later joined the **Hound Group** of the **American Kennel Club**.

Today, people still love these popular pets!

Happy Hounds

Bassets can be loud and silly. They like to make friends with other pets and children.

They can also be lazy.
Bassets like to take naps!

These dogs also like to go on walks. They follow their noses everywhere.

Bassets explore the world
one scent at a time!

Glossary

American Kennel Club—an organization that keeps track of dog breeds in the United States

bi-color—a color that has two fur colors, with one being white

bred—purposely mated two dogs to make puppies with certain qualities

breed—a type of dog

coats—the hair or fur covering some animals

droopy—saggy and hanging down

glossy—shiny and smooth

Hound Group—a group of dog breeds that often have a history of hunting

lemon—a light tan color

scents—odors and smells

stocky—having a solid, heavy body

tri-color—a pattern that has three colors

To Learn More

AT THE LIBRARY

Gagne, Tammy. *Foxhounds, Coonhounds, and Other Hound Dogs.* North Mankato, Minn.: Capstone Press, 2017.

Gray, Susan H. *Basset Hounds.* New York, N.Y.: AV2 by Weigl, 2017.

Schuh, Mari. *Beagles.* Minneapolis, Minn.: Bellwether Media, 2016.

ON THE WEB

Learning more about basset hounds is as easy as 1, 2, 3.

1. Go to www.factsurfer.com.

2. Enter "basset hounds" into the search box.

3. Click the "Surf" button and you will see a list of related web sites.

With factsurfer.com, finding more information is just a click away.

Index

The images in this book are reproduced through the courtesy of: Susan Schmitz, front cover; sanjagrujic, p. 4; Dr. Alan Lipkin, pp. 4-5, 15; Trybex, pp. 6-7; GeptaYs, p. 7; BehindTheLens, pp. 8-9; cynoclub, p. 9 (left); Eric Isselee, pp. 9 (center, right), 12; mountainberryphoto/ Getty Images, p. 10; f8grapher, p. 11; John Robertson/ Alamy, pp. 12-13; Daleen Loest, pp. 14-15; Zuzule, p. 16; Alvaro Pantoja, p. 17; VStock/ Alamy, p. 18; pranee mankit, pp. 18-19; DLILLC/ Corbis/ VCG/ Getty Images, p. 20; lienkie, p. 21.